Passion Unleashed: Igniting The Future With Purpose.

Carl Davis

Published by Carl Davis, 2024.

PASSION UNLEASHED: IGNITING THE FUTURE WITH PURPOSE.

First edition. February 27, 2024.

ISBN: 979-8224238521

Written by Carl Davis.

Also by Carl Davis

Ek, is Dawid Soeker

A Brief History Of Christianity In Africa

Icing the Eskimo - The Art of Aggressive Sales

Introduction to Pastoral Counselling

Nuclear Faith

Toxic Pulpit

Van Paradegrond tot Pastorie

Group Dynamics and Motivation

Introduction to Leadership and Management

Pastoral counselling models for perinatal and postpartum episodes

Basic New Testament Survey

Help! I'm managing personnel

So......You want to be a Waiter

The Art of Preaching

Eternal Logos: The Evolution of Scriptural Interpretation: From Ancient Methodology to Postmodern Perspectives

Ewige Woord Die Evolusie van Skrifuitleg: Van Antieke Metodiek tot Postmoderne Perspektiewe

Teaching Ministry

The Funny Side Of Reasoning - Fallacies, principles and typologies in the modern business world.

Passion Unleashed: Igniting The Future With Purpose.

Table of Contents

"Passion Unleashed: Igniting the Future with Purpose!"

Dr. Carl J Davis
East London, South Africa
2024

The History of Passion

Identifying and studying the concept of "passion" within psychology has a rich history spanning a variety of psychological traditions and paradigms. This broad-lined chapter will give an overview of the development of the concept of passion within psychology, highlighting several vital psychologists and their approaches to the topic.

Early History of the Concept of Passion

The concept of passion has a long history in the human experience and has accepted various forms and meanings over the centuries. In ancient Greek philosophy, passion was associated with the emotional afflictions of the human soul, such as love, desire, and suffering. The Platonic and Aristotelian traditions each offered a unique perspective on passion, with Plato viewing passion as an irrational urge to be controlled by reason and Aristotle viewing passion as an essential part of human nature to be balanced by virtue.

The Influence of Christian Theology

Christian theology had an essential influence on passion, especially in the Middle Ages and the Renaissance. In Christian thought, passion was often viewed as human nature's propensity for sin and desire to be governed by the religious virtues of faith, hope, and love. Medieval theologians such as Augustine and Thomas of Aquinas offered a deep insight into the nature of passion within a theological framework.

The Enlightenment and the Rise of Modern Psychology

The Age of Enlightenment brought a shift in thinking about passion with the emergence of modern psychology as a distinct scientific discipline. Early modern psychologists, such as René Descartes and Baruch Spinoza, began viewing passion as an objective phenomenon that could be studied and understood through scientific methods.

The Romantic Movement and the Emotional Revolution

The Romantic movement in the 19th century brought about a reappraisal of passion as a central aspect of the human experience.

Romantic writers, philosophers, and artists emphasized the intensity and depth of human emotions, which influenced psychology's development. Psychologists like William James began exploring the human experience's emotional dimensions. They saw passion as a critical component of a meaningful life.

The Freudian Revolution and the Role of Passion in the Unconscious

Sigmund Freud's theory of the unconscious profoundly influenced how passion is viewed within psychology. Freud emphasized the role of passion in the unconscious and viewed passion as a critical source of emotional energy and conflict within the human soul. His theories of libido, sexuality, and the id further explored the nature of passion within psychology.

The Humanist Revolution and the Idea of Self-Realization

Humanistic psychology, especially the work of Carl Rogers and Abraham Maslow, brought a new perspective to passion as a source of self-realization and personal growth. Humanistic psychologists consider passion an essential aspect of human nature motivated by the pursuit of self-realization and potential fulfillment.

The Cognitive Revolution and the Understanding of Motivation

The cognitive revolution in psychology brought about a further development of the concept of passion, primarily through the understanding of motivation and goal setting. Psychologists such as Albert Bandura and Martin Seligman have begun to explore the cognitive aspects of passion, including the role of self-efficacy, self-concept, and self-motivation.

The Contemporary Perspectives on Passion

In contemporary psychology, passion is viewed as a complex emotional, cognitive, and behavioral phenomenon encompassing many factors. Modern psychologists, such as Mihaly Csikszentmihalyi, Carol Dweck, and Angela Duckworth, have begun to explore the dynamics of passion in multiple contexts, including the workplace, education, and personal relationships.

Concluding view

The development of the concept of passion within psychology is a complex and dynamic process involving a wide range of psychological traditions and paradigms. From ancient philosophy to contemporary psychology, several psychologists have contributed to our understanding of the role of passion in the human experience. This diversity of perspectives and approaches provided a rich and nuanced picture of passion as a critical aspect of human nature.

Modern take on Passion

The modern view of passion within psychology has evolved dramatically over the past few decades due to the emergence of new theoretical frameworks, research methods, and areas of application. These modern perspectives have brought about a deeper understanding of the dynamics and impact of passion in various areas of life, including work, school, personal relationships, and other activities. Below, we will provide an overview of the modern view of passion within psychology regarding various psychological theorists, research findings, and areas of application.

Self-determination theory (SDT)

Self-Determination Theory, developed by Edward Deci and Richard Ryan, provides an essential framework for studying intrinsic motivation and passion. According to SDT, passion is an intrinsic motivating force that comes from the self-determination of pursuing personal goals. The theory distinguishes between three forms of motivation: intrinsic, identified, and extrapolated. Passion is a form of intrinsic motivation that arises from the experience of freedom, self-determination, and purposefulness.

Self-Determination Theory (SDT) is a leading theoretical framework within psychology that focuses on the dynamics of human motivation and behavior, especially regarding the distinction between intrinsic and extrinsic motivation. SDT was developed by Edward Deci and Richard Ryan in the early 1980s and has since played a highly influential role in several application areas within psychology, including education, work, health care, and personal development.

Basic Concepts of Self-Determination Theory

The Need for Self-Determination

The core concept of SDT is the need for self-determination, which refers to the inherent desire of individuals to steer and control their own actions and behaviors. These include a sense of freedom, freedom of choice, and self-management. SDT emphasizes that satisfying this basic need is essential for promoting human well-being and purposefulness.

Intrinsic and extrinsic motivation

SDT distinguishes between two types of motivation that can lead people to undertake action: intrinsic and extrinsic.

- **Intrinsic Motivation:** This type of motivation arises from internal factors such as personal interest, satisfaction, and self-goals. When an individual is intrinsically motivated to do a particular activity, they do it because they enjoy it and derive intrinsic satisfaction.

- **Extrinsic Motivation:** Unlike intrinsic motivation, extrinsic motivation arises from external factors such as rewards, punishment, and the need for approval or success. When an extrinsically motivated person do an activity he does so for external rewards or to avoid negative consequences rather than from an inner interest or satisfaction.

The Continuum of Self-Determination

SDT suggests that there is a continuum of self-determination, reflecting varying degrees of motivation, from low self-determination to high self-determination:

- **Motivation:** The lowest level of the continuum refers to a lack of motivation or interest in a particular activity. This is when a person has no apparent reason to exhibit a specific behavior.

- **External Regulation:** An extrinsic motivation where the individual exhibits behavior due to external rewards or pressures, such as the expectation of rewards or the fear of punishment.

- **Identified Regulation:** A more internalized form of extrinsic motivation where the individual exhibits a behavior because they recognize its value and identify with the goals it serves.

- **Integrated Regulation:** An even more internalized form of extrinsic motivation where the behavior is integrated with the individual's values and identity.
- **Identity volunteerism:** The highest level of the continuum, reflecting intrinsic motivation, where the individual exhibits a behavior because it is an integral part of their self-identity and values.

Application Areas of Self-Determination Theory

SDT has vast implications for several areas of application within psychology and other fields:

- **Education:** In education, SDT focuses on promoting intrinsic motivation and self-determination through pupil-oriented approaches that encourage the learner's freedom of choice and self-management.
- **Work environment:** In the workplace context, SDT applies to promoting self-determination, self-motivation, and job satisfaction by creating a supportive environment that satisfies the employee's intrinsic needs.
- **Healthcare:** In healthcare applications, SDT is used to understand the motivation for health-promoting behaviors and to develop interventions that promote the self-determination of individuals to make healthy choices.
- **Personal Development:** On a personal level, SDT can promote self-motivation and self-determination through a better understanding of intrinsic needs and goals.

Criticism and Further Developments

Although Self-Determination Theory is a rich and influential framework, it is not without criticism. Some points of criticism include the tendency of the theory to focus primarily on Western cultural contexts and to consider the possibility of cultural variation in the expression of self-determination. Furthermore, there is debate about the theory's practical implications in various application areas, including education and workplace management.

Despite these criticisms, Self-Determination Theory remains an essential and influential framework for studying human motivation and behavior, and it remains a source of insight and inspiration for researchers and practitioners striving for a better understanding of human well-being and purposefulness.

Cognitive Evaluation Theory (CET)

Cognitive Evaluation Theory, proposed by Robert White, investigates the dynamics of passion in evaluating activities in terms of their intrinsic and extrinsic value. According to CET, passion is influenced by subjective perceptions of activities, including the degree to which an individual views an activity as interesting, enjoyable, and essential. These subjective evaluations determine the degree of engagement and passion an individual experiences in a particular activity.

This theory originated in the fifties, when there was an increasing interest in the interaction between emotions and cognition, and it made a valuable contribution to understanding how individuals evaluate and respond to their environment.

Basic Concepts of Cognitive Evaluation Theory

Evaluation of Activities

One of the fundamental concepts of CET is the idea that individuals evaluate an activity or situation by the degree of intrinsic and extrinsic value it has for them. This evaluation is subjective and may be influenced by individual perceptions, experiences, and values.

Intrinsic and extrinsic value

According to CET, an individual may consider an activity intrinsically valuable if it is inherently interesting, enjoyable, or meaningful to them. On the other hand, an activity may have extrinsic value due to external factors such as rewards, approval, or the avoidance of punishment.

Contextual Evaluation

CET also emphasizes the importance of the context in which an activity takes place. This means that the same activity can be evaluated differently depending on the individual's circumstances and unique characteristics. This contextual evaluation contributes to the dynamic nature of emotional responses and motivation.

Emotional reactions

Evaluating an activity or situation directly impacts an individual's emotional responses. Suppose an activity is evaluated as valuable and satisfying. In that case, it will likely bring about positive emotional reactions, such as happiness and satisfaction. Conversely, suppose an activity is evaluated as unpleasant or unimportant. In that case, it can cause adverse emotional reactions, such as dissatisfaction and frustration.

Motivational Implications

The evaluation of activities also has direct implications for the motivation of individuals. If an activity is evaluated as intrinsically valuable, there is a higher level of self-motivation. On the other hand, a decrease in intrinsic value can lead to a reduction in self-motivation.

Application Areas of Cognitive Evaluation Theory

Cognitive Evaluation Theory has a variety of application areas within psychology, including:

- **Education:** In the education context, CET can be used to understand how students evaluate their learning activities and how this evaluation affects their motivation to learn.
- **Work environment:** In the workplace context, CET applies to evaluating work tasks and their impact on employees' emotional responses and job satisfaction.
- **Healthcare:** In healthcare applications, CET can be used to

study the perceptions of health practices and how these perceptions impact patients' motivation to adopt healthy behaviors.

- **Culture and Society:** CET may also be applied to examine the cultural and societal influences on the evaluation of activities and how this evaluation affects the behavior of individuals in a community.

Criticism and Further Developments

CET is not without criticism, and one of the criticisms is that it may be too simple and does not address the full complexity of emotional and motivational processes. Some researchers have indicated a need for a more nuanced approach that examines the interaction of cognition and emotions in more depth.

Despite the criticisms, Cognitive Evaluation Theory remains a valuable framework for studying how individuals evaluate their environment, experience emotional reactions, and are motivated. This contributes to a holistic understanding of the interaction between cognition, emotion, and behavior within multiple contexts.

Self-Concept Theories (SCT)

Self-concept theories, developed by Hazel Markus and Saul Rosenburg, emphasize the importance of self-concept in the emergence and expression of passion. According to SCT, passion is intertwined with an individual's self-concept and the perceptions of self-worth and self-efficacy. A strong self-concept can lead to a more profound identification with and involvement in passionate activities. In contrast, a weak self-concept can lead to a lack of self-motivation and purposefulness.

Self-concept theories (SCT) are an essential theoretical framework within psychology that focuses on the role of self-concepts in shaping behavior, emotions, and well-being. The theory originated in the 1970s and has since greatly influenced several application areas within psychology, including personality theory, clinical psychology, and social psychology.

Basic Concepts of Self-Concept Theories

Self-concept

The core concept of SCT is the self-concept, which refers to the subjective perceptions and beliefs an individual has about himself or herself. These include aspects such as self-worth, self-efficacy, and self-esteem. The self-concept is a dynamic entity formed by an interplay of internal and external factors, including personal experiences, social interactions, and cultural influences.

Self-constructions

SCT emphasizes that self-concepts consist of multiple self-constructions or dimensions representing different aspects of the self. These constructions may vary depending on the context and may include, among others:

- **Self-worth:** The degree to which an individual values and respects himself or herself.
- **Self-efficacy:** The conviction of an individual in their ability to perform specific tasks or challenges.
- **Self-esteem:** The perceptions and beliefs an individual has about their characteristics, characteristics, and identity.
- **Self-ideals:** The ideal images and aspirations an individual has for himself or herself.

Continuity and Change

SCT emphasizes that self-concepts tend to be relatively stable over time. Still, they can also be subject to change and adaptation due to experiences, interactions, and developmental events.

There is an ongoing interplay between the existing self-concepts and new experiences that contribute to the formation and adaptation of the self-concept over time.

Self-consistency and self-congruence

SCT suggests that individuals have an inherent need for self-consistency and self-resemblance, which refers to the longing to make their perceptions and beliefs match their behaviors and experiences. A dissonance between an individual's self-concepts and their behavior or experiences can lead to emotional tension and a drive for self-consistency to reduce this tension.

Cultural and contextual differences

SCT also recognizes the influence of cultural and contextual factors on self-concepts. Self-concepts are formed within a specific social and cultural context. They can, therefore, vary between different cultural groups and contexts. The value and meaning attached to different self-constructions may also vary depending on the culture and context in which an individual finds himself or herself.

Application Areas of Self-Concept Theories

SCT has a wide range of application areas within psychology, including:

- **Personality Development:** SCT provides insight into the development of self-concepts over time and how these concepts contribute to forming personality and identity.
- **Clinical Psychology:** In the clinical psychological context, SCT can be used to explore the role of self-concepts in emotional well-being, self-esteem, and personal growth.
- **Social Psychology:** SCT provides insight into the social determinants of self-concepts and how social interactions and identification with groups shape the self-concept.

Criticism and Further Developments

While SCT is a valuable framework for studying self-concepts, the theory also has criticisms. Some researchers emphasize that the theory may be oversimplified and does not address the full complexity of self-concepts and their formation. There is a need for further research to investigate the dynamics and diversity of self-concepts in various contexts.

Despite these critical points, Self-Concept Theories remain an essential and influential framework for studying self-concepts and their impact on behavior, emotions, and well-being. This contributes to a better understanding of the subjective perceptions and beliefs that shape the self and provides a valuable lens for studying personality, identity, and social interactions.

Emotional Intelligence (EI)

Emotional Intelligence, developed by Daniel Goleman, provides a framework for understanding the role of emotions in the emergence and expression of passion. According to EI, passion is intertwined with an individual's emotional intelligence, including recognizing, understanding, and managing emotions. A high level of emotional intelligence can lead to a more profound ability to navigate passionate emotions and use them as a source of energy and motivation.

Emotional Intelligence (EI) was developed in the 1990s. It refers to the ability to recognize, understand, use, and manage emotions, both in one's own emotions and other people's emotions. EI has played an essential role in studying human behavior and well-being, particularly in the context of personal and professional development.

Basic Concepts of Emotional Intelligence

Emotional Awareness

Emotional awareness is the ability to recognize and understand one's own emotions, as well as the ability to identify emotional reactions in various situations.

It involves an awareness of one's emotional state and the ability to identify these emotions without judging them.

Emotional control

Emotional control refers to the ability to manage and regulate one's emotions effectively, including promoting positive emotions and reducing negative ones. It involves managing stressful situations, controlling anger, and promoting calm and well-being.

Emotional empathy

Emotional empathy involves the ability to recognize, understand, and feel other people's emotions. This includes the ability to understand the perspectives of others and to show compassion and sympathy in response to their emotional states.

Emotional intelligence in relationships

Emotional intelligence plays a critical role in developing and maintaining healthy relationships. It involves communicating effectively, maintaining emotional boundaries, and providing empathy and support to others in a relationship.

Emotional intelligence in work environments

EI is particularly important for leadership, collaboration, and employee relationships in the work environment. Leaders with high EI are often better equipped to foster a positive work culture, manage conflicts effectively, and motivate employees.

Areas of Emotional Intelligence

- **Education:** EI has applications in the education environment, particularly for promoting positive interactions between teachers and students, addressing behavior problems, and promoting academic success.
- **Business Environments:** In the business environment, EI is essential in leadership, teamwork, and customer service. EI can contribute to developing influential leaders, fostering collaboration and team communication, and creating a positive customer experience.
- **Healthcare:** In healthcare settings, EI can contribute to better patient relationships, foster collaboration between healthcare teams, and address emotional challenges in healthcare practice.
- **Personal Development:** On a personal level, EI can contribute

to a better understanding of one's own emotions, promoting self-awareness and self-control and developing healthy relationships with other people.

Criticism and Further Developments

While EI is a valuable concept, there are also criticisms of its measurement and application. Some researchers have suggested that the idea is too subjective and difficult to measure, and there is a need for further research to improve the method of measurement and explain the relationship between EI and other personality traits.

Despite these criticisms, Emotional Intelligence remains an essential concept for studying human behavior and well-being, especially in the context of personal and professional development. It provides a valuable framework for promoting self-awareness, interpersonal skills, and healthy relationships.

Positive Psychology

Positive Psychology, an emerging field within psychology, focuses on promoting well-being, self-realization, and positive human experiences, including passion. Positive psychologists such as Martin Seligman and Mihaly Csikszentmihalyi emphasize the importance of living out passion as a key to a fulfilled life. This approach promotes positive emotions, engagement, and performance in pursuing passions and goals.

Areas of application

Modern views of passion within psychology have also had an impact on several areas of application, including:

- **Career Development:** Studying passion in the workplace has contributed to a better understanding of the role of passion in career development, job satisfaction, and career achievement. Career counseling programs and interventions often use a passion-oriented approach to help individuals make career choices that will make them feel engaged and fulfilled.

- **Education:** Passion plays a vital role in students' learning experiences and achievements. Education practitioners and educators often use a passion-oriented approach to help students identify and develop their unique interests and strengths.
- **Personal Growth:** On a personal level, passion plays a critical role in promoting self-realization and personal growth. Personal development programs and interventions often promote passionate activities and identify personal passions as a key to a fulfilled life.

Positive psychology is a branch of psychology that focuses on studying positive experiences, traits, and processes that contribute to human well-being and thriving lives. This represents a shift from the traditional psychological focus on problems, pathologies, and disorders towards a more holistic approach that promotes positive emotional, cognitive, and social functioning.

The concept of positive psychology has developed in the last few decades as a response to the growing interest in promoting human well-being, happiness, and thriving lives.

Core Principles of Positive Psychology

Focus on Wellness and Thriving Lives

Positive psychology focuses on identifying and promoting well-being and thriving lives rather than diagnosing and treating pathologies and disorders. This includes studying positive experiences such as happiness, satisfaction, and meaningful lives and promoting resilience and positive development.

Examination of Positive Emotional, Cognitive, and Social Characteristics

Positive psychology explores a range of positive emotional, cognitive, and social attributes that contribute to well-being and thriving lives.

These include optimism, self-efficacy, gratitude, resilience, altruism, and empathy.

The Role of Positive Emotions

An essential aspect of positive psychology is the role of positive emotions, such as happiness, joy, peace, and contentment, in promoting well-being and thriving lives. Positive emotions are considered an essential indicator of well-being. They can have a positive influence on health, relationships, and performance.

Promoting Leadership and Personal Growth

Positive psychology emphasizes promoting leadership and personal growth as an essential goal for individuals and communities. This includes self-awareness, acceptance, mastery, and pursuing meaningful goals.

The Role of Positive Relationships

Positive psychology explores the critical role of positive relationships in promoting well-being and thriving lives. These include fostering intimate relationships, supportive social networks, and positive social interactions.

Areas of Application of Positive Psychology

Positive psychology has many application areas within psychology and other fields. These include the following:

Clinical Psychology: In the clinical psychological context, positive psychology promotes well-being and thriving lives among individuals struggling with emotional difficulties and challenges. These include promoting resilience, self-efficacy, and positive cognition.

Education: Positive psychology promotes positive development and well-being among learners and educators in the education environment. This includes promoting self-efficacy, motivation, and academic achievement.

Business Environments: Positive psychology promotes well-being and productivity among employees and organizations in the business environment. This includes fostering leadership, employee engagement, and positive work environments.

Health care: Positive psychology promotes health and well-being among patients and healthcare workers in the healthcare environment. This includes promoting self-care, emotional well-being, and patient satisfaction.

Criticism and Further Developments

Despite the growing interest in positive psychology, its concept and application are also criticized. Some researchers emphasize that positive psychology may be oversimplified and does not address the full complexity of human experiences and behaviors. There is a need for further research to understand the relationship between positive and negative aspects of human well-being and the application of positive psychology in different cultural and contextual settings.

Despite these criticisms, positive psychology remains an essential and influential branch of psychology that promotes well-being, happiness, and thriving lives. It offers an alternative approach to studying human behavior that encourages positive experiences and qualities, contributing to a meaningful and fulfilled life.

In conjunction with the above-mentioned theoretical frameworks and areas of application, modern views of passion within psychology have achieved a comprehensive and nuanced understanding of the dynamics and impact of passion in the human experience. This approach offered a deeper insight into the importance of passion for well-being, fulfillment, and success in various areas of life.

Let's get passionate.....

Define passion: Start by defining the concept of passion and exploring what it means to different people. Passion can take various forms, including personal passions such as creativity, sport, and knowledge, and professional passions such as career development and societal impact.

The Importance of Passion: Explore the importance of passion in an individual's life. Discuss how passion can contribute to a sense of purpose, self-realization, and overall happiness. Also, you can examine the negative consequences of living without passion, such as feelings of emptiness, dissatisfaction, and lack of motivation.

Discovering Passion: Give clues and tips on how people might find their passions. These can include self-reflection exercises, trying new activities and interests, and identifying what people feel passionate about.

The Power of Research and Experimentation: Encourage readers to explore their passions by researching, experimenting, and moving out of their comfort zone. This could include learning new skills, participating in activities they've never done, and seeking mentorship and guidance from others who share their passions.

Overcoming Challenges and Obstacles: Identify the challenges and barriers people may encounter in pursuing their passions, such as time, finances, and self-doubt. Present practical strategies and motivational stories to overcome these barriers.

The integration of passion into life:

The ongoing journey of passion:

A new dimension that can be explored is the role of passion in community building and social impact.

The role of passion in community building and social impact is a critical factor that can profoundly impact the development and well-being of communities worldwide. Passion is a solid emotional and motivating force that drives individuals to devote their time, energy, and resources to causes and projects they believe in and for which they have a true passion.

Channeling this passion into community initiatives and social impact projects can catalyze positive change and growth within a community.

Passion as a Motivating Force

Passion is a powerful motivating driver for individuals to engage in community-building and social impact activities.

When people have a deep passion for a particular cause, they feel passionate and motivated to take action to make a difference.

This drive can lead to higher engagement, commitment, and persistence in community projects.

Positive Impact of Passion on Community Building

Strengthening Community Identity

Expressing passion by individuals for their community and executing projects that feed their passion can foster a strong sense of community identity.

When people get involved in matters they have passion for, it creates a sense of connectedness and cooperation within the community.

Promoting Social Cooperation and Cooperation

Passion can foster social cooperation and collaboration between individuals and groups within a community. The shared passion for a cause can unite people and encourage them to work together to achieve common goals.

This cohesion can lead to joint initiatives and projects that benefit the community.

Development of Human Capital

Expressing passion through community engagement and social impact activities can lead to human capital development within a community.

Individuals who pursue their passion through community building can develop skills, experiences, and networks that not only promote personal growth but also increase the overall well-being of the community.

Stimulating Innovation and Creativity

Passion can be a catalyst for innovation and creativity within a community. When people are motivated by their passion, it can encourage them to explore new ideas, try new approaches, and develop innovative solutions to common challenges.

Limitations and Challenges

While the role of passion in community building and social impact can be substantial, it is crucial to recognize that there are limitations and challenges as well. Some of these challenges include:

- **Unequal Access:** Not everyone has equal access to resources and opportunities to pursue their passions, which can result in unequal participation in community building and social impact projects.
- **Burnout:** Excessive involvement in passion-driven projects can lead to burnout and exhaustion, especially if individuals do not balance their personal and community obligations.
- **Internal Conflicts:** Differences in opinions and values within a community can lead to internal conflicts and divisions, undermining the effectiveness of passion-driven projects.

Fostering Passion in Community Building

To promote the role of passion in community building and social impact, it is vital to create an environment that encourages and supports the expression of passion. This includes promoting community awareness, providing opportunities for engagement and participation, and creating supportive networks and resources for individuals who want to pursue their passion for the betterment of the community.

At its core, passion in community building and social impact contributes to creating a more resilient, collaborative and thriving community that positively impacts the well-being of all its members.

Motivational Stories On Passion

Here are some personal stories, anecdotes, and practical examples that can inspire people's passions:

The Lost Artist: Sara knew all her life that she had a passion for art but never took it seriously. It was just a recreational activity for her. But one day, after visiting an exhibition of local artists, she realized her deep love for art. She decided to take an art atelier and started her own paintings. Today, she is a successful artist who follows her passion and exhibits her work in several galleries.

The Music Enthusiast: Johan always had a passion for music but never thought he could pursue it as a career. After years of an office job that made him unhappy, he took his passion for music seriously. He started taking music lessons and eventually built a successful career as a musician and composer. Now, he enjoys every day of his work and feels fulfilled by his passion.

The Adventurous Traveler: Emily always had a passion for travel, but she never thought it would be possible to make it a part of her life. After years of ordinary office life, she chose a career that would allow her to explore the world. She started a blog to share her travel adventures and eventually built a successful career as a travel blogger. Today, she travels the world, inspiring others to follow their own travel passions.

These personal stories illustrate how people can discover and follow their passions, even when it seems discouraging or impossible at first. Through self-discovery, courage, and perseverance, anyone can tap into their passions and build a fulfilling life based on the things they love most.

Author's And Passion

A variety of writers and thinkers can contribute inspiring insights and ideas to the topic. Here are some authors you can quote and use their work to further explore the concept of passion:

Cheryl Strayed is the author of the memoir "Wild: From Lost to Found on the Pacific Crest Trail," which also chronicles a personal journey of challenges, growth, and self-discovery.

In "Wild," Strayed tells the story of her own journey on the Pacific Crest Trail after experiencing a painful divorce, the death of her mother, and a period of self-destruction. Her journey of more than 1,100 miles on foot through the wilderness of the Pacific Crest Trail marks her search for healing, meaning, and self-discovery. Like Gilbert, Strayed shares her personal experiences and emotions sincerely and honestly, and her story of self-growth and ultimate enlightenment will touch a broader public's hearts.

By choosing Cheryl Strayed in place of Elizabeth Gilbert, readers will experience a different but equally powerful story of self-discovery, which can also profoundly impact how they look at their own lives. Strayed's candid narrative and deep humanity make her an ideal choice for readers who want to embark on a journey of self-discovery but with a different perspective and life experience than Gilbert's.

Brené Brown: Brené Brown's work on hurtfulness, courage, and connectedness can offer insights into how passion is associated with taking risks and embracing vulnerability. Her books, such as "Daring Greatly" and "The Gifts of Imperfection" can serve as inspirational sources.

"The Gifts of Imperfection: Let Go of Who You Think You're Supposed to Be and Embrace Who You Are" is a self-help book by Brené Brown, a renowned research coach in human emotional well-being and acceptance. In this book, published in 2010, Brown explores the concept of perfectionism and how it prevents us from connecting fully and in a healthy way with ourselves and others.

The book is divided into three parts: "Let Go of Who You Think You Should Be," "Accept Who You Are," and "Live Wholeheartedly". In each part, Brown explores a critical aspect of self-acceptance and personal growth.

Part One: Let Go of Who You Think You Should Be

In the book's first part, Brown explores the influence of perfectionism and the culture of "must" on our lives. She highlights the harmful effects of perfectionism on our self-esteem, relationships, and overall well-being. By exploring the idea of "must" and the pressure to meet an unattainable standard, Brown encourages readers to recognize and change the critical voice in their own heads.

Brown proposes several practical strategies for letting go of perfectionism and freeing the critical voice, including practicing self-compassion, identifying one's values, and accepting vulnerability as a source of power.

Part Two: Accept Who You Are

In the book's second part, Brown explores the concepts of self-acceptance and self-love. She stresses the importance of accepting yourself just as you are, with all your faults, flaws, and unique qualities. By cultivating the practice of self-compassion and compassionate self-talk, readers can cultivate a more profound sense of self-acceptance and develop a more positive relationship with their own selves.

Brown encourages readers to recognize the value of vulnerability and be honest about their feelings and experiences. She suggests that vulnerability is not a shortcoming but a source of power and connection to others.

Part Three: Live Wholeheartedly

In the book's third part, Brown focuses on the concept of "living wholeheartedly" and how to live a life that aligns with our values and passions. She stresses the importance of setting boundaries, taking good care of ourselves, and actively working towards a meaningful and fulfilling life.

Brown encourages readers to embrace their creative forms of expression and find joy in the things they are passionate about. She suggests that by living a life that aligns with our values and interests, we can find the most profound joy and fulfillment.

In "The Gifts of Imperfection," Brené Brown offers a powerful message of self-acceptance, self-compassion, and wholehearted living. She encourages readers to let go of perfectionism and the critical voice in their own heads and instead live a life that aligns with their values and passions. The book offers a practical and in-depth look at how to live a more fulfilled and happy life through a deeper relationship with ourselves and others.

Daniel H. Pink: Pink's book "Drive: The Surprising Truth About What Motivates Us" explores the role of intrinsic motivation and passion in our work and lives. His ideas about the importance of self-determination, mastery, and meaningfulness in our pursuit may be relevant to a book about passion.

"Drive: The Surprising Truth About What Motivates Us" is a book by Daniel H. Pink, published in 2009. This book explores the true nature of motivation and focuses mainly on intrinsic and extrinsic motivation.

Pink uses a combination of research, personal anecdotes, and practical examples to offer an insightful look at what motivates people in the workplace and beyond.

Part One: The Cognitive Knowledge

In the book's first part, Pink highlights the limitations of traditional economic theories that assume people are motivated by external rewards, such as money. He calls this type of motivation "extrinsic motivation." He argues that it is often insufficient to promote long-term motivation and engagement. Pink argues that a new approach to motivation that recognizes the importance of intrinsic motivation is needed.

Part Two: The Three Elements

In the book's second part, Pink identifies the three elements that drive intrinsic motivation: autonomy, mastery, and sense. He discusses these elements in detail and illustrates their critical role in promoting self-driven behavior.

Autonomy: This refers to the need for individuals to have some degree of self-management about their own lives and work. Pink argues that promoting independence in the workplace can lead to an improved sense of ownership and engagement at work.

Mastery: This refers to the desire to develop a skill or achieve a challenging goal, yet within the reach of an individual's abilities. Pink argues that the possibility of growing and advancing in a skill can be a powerful motivating force.

Sence: It refers to the longing to be part of something greater than ourselves and have a meaningful purpose. Pink argues that fostering sense in the workplace can lead to a greater sense of accomplishment and satisfaction in employees.

Part Three: The Vicissitudes

In the book's third part, Pink discusses the implications of this new view of motivation for the workplace and how it can be applied to create a more fulfilled and productive work culture. He also offers practical tips for individuals and organizations to embrace the principles of intrinsic motivation.

Pink's message is that people are motivated by external rewards and the more profound need for autonomy, mastery, and sense. By recognizing and meeting these needs, organizations can create an environment where employees are more engaged and fulfilled.

In "Drive," Daniel H. Pink sheds new light on motivation by emphasizing the importance of intrinsic motivation. By shifting the focus from external rewards to the need for autonomy, mastery, and sense, Pink provides a deeper understanding of what motivates people and how to create an environment that encourages them to do their best work. This is a book that can have an impact on individuals and organizations striving for a more fulfilled and productive life and workplace.

Angela Duckworth: Duckworth is known for her concept of "grit" and its role in success. Her book "Grit: The Power of Passion and Perseverance" explores how passion and perseverance go hand in hand to help us achieve our goals.

"Grit: The Power of Passion and Perseverance" is a book by Angela Duckworth and published in 2016. This book explores the concept of "grit," which Duckworth defines as a combination of passion and perseverance, and how it plays a vital role in success and achievement. Through research, personal stories, and practical examples, Duckworth sheds light on the importance of grit in our personal and professional lives. Here is a summary of the main themes and ideas in "Grit":

Part One: What is Grit?

In the book's first part, Duckworth defines the concept of "grit" and explores how it comes to be and is developed. She argues that grit consists of two crucial components: passion and perseverance.

Passion is a deep interest and commitment to a specific goal or activity. In contrast, perseverance refers to the ability to persevere and persevere even in the face of challenges and failure.

Duckworth suggests that grit is not just an innate trait but something developed through hard work, practice, and multifaceted experience. She explores the role of environmental factors, such as parenting, education, and community environments, in fostering grit, emphasizing the importance of self-discovery and experimentation in shaping passions and goals.

Part Two: Grit in Practice

In the book's second part, Duckworth offers practical tips and strategies for developing grit in our own lives. She discusses the role of goal setting, practice, and persistence in promoting grit, encouraging readers to focus on long-term goals and embrace hard work and perseverance.

Duckworth illustrates these concepts with various practical examples, including the life stories of successful people who see grit as a critical component of their accomplishments. She stresses the importance of self-control and a positive, growth-oriented mindset in fostering grit. She encourages readers to see failure as an opportunity for growth and learning.

Part Three: Grit in the Workplace and Education

In the book's third part, Duckworth explores the implications of grit for the workplace and education. She argues that grit plays a critical role in successful careers and academic achievements and provides a range of practical recommendations for promoting grit in these environments.

Duckworth stresses the importance of a culture of grit in the workplace and school, encouraging leaders and educators to create an environment that promotes and rewards passion and perseverance. She suggests that success depends not only on intelligence or talent but also on the ability to work hard and persevere, even when things get tough.

"Grit: The Power of Passion and Perseverance" is a book that offers an insightful look at the importance of grit in our personal and professional lives. Angela Duckworth highlights the concept of grit as a critical factor in success and achievement. She offers practical tips and strategies for developing this crucial trait. This book encourages readers to follow their passions, work hard, and never give up because grit can be the key to long-term success and fulfillment.

Carol Dweck: Dweck's work on the growth mindset and the importance of a positive approach to mistakes and challenges may also be relevant to a study in passion. Her book "Mindset: The New Psychology of Success" offers insights into how our attitudes and beliefs influence our ability to follow our passions.

"Mindset: The New Psychology of Success" is a book written by Carol S. Dweck, a leading psychologist who explores the concept of "mindset" and how it impacts success, achievement, and personal growth. This book, published in 2006, offers an insightful look at the two main types of mindsets, namely a "fixed" mindset and a "growth" mindset, and how they affect our behavior, thinking, and performance.

The Concept of Mindset

At the heart of "Mindset" is the idea that our thinking about our abilities greatly impacts our life and achievements. Dweck argues two main types of mindsets: a "fixed" mindset and a "growth" mindset. A fixed mindset is when people believe their abilities, intelligence, and talents are captured and cannot change. On the other hand, a growth mindset is when a person believes that their abilities can be developed through dedication, hard work, and learning.

Dweck emphasizes that the type of mindset we adopt greatly impacts our behavior, choices, and ultimate success. For example, a person with a fixed mindset may be afraid to take risks or take on challenges because they fear failing and doubt their intelligence or talent. On the other hand, a person with a growth mindset would rather welcome challenges than see opportunities for growth and development.

The Effects of Different Mindsets

In "Mindset," Dweck explores the effects of these different mindsets on various areas, including academics, sports, business, and personal relationships. She points out that a growth mindset often leads to more multifaceted, sustainable success. In contrast, a fixed mindset often leads to stagnation and a fear of failure.

For example, in the academic world, learners with a growth mindset may be more likely to take challenging courses and push themselves to improve. In contrast, learners with a fixed mindset may tend to limit themselves to subjects they are already familiar with and restrict themselves to a particular level of achievement.

In the business world, a growth mindset can lead to more innovative thinking and an ability to take risks and tackle challenges. In contrast, a fixed mindset can lead to stagnation and a lack of adaptive capacity in a changing environment.

The Role of Education and Education

Dweck also discusses the role of education in fostering a growth mindset. She stresses the importance of a culture that welcomes mistakes and failures as opportunities for growth and learning. Teachers can play a critical role in fostering a growth mindset by creating an environment where learners are encouraged to take on challenges and push themselves to improve.

Developing a Growth Mindset

"Mindset" also offers practical tips and strategies for developing a growth mindset. Dweck encourages readers to explore their thinking about their abilities and to recognize and replace negative self-talk and limiting beliefs with positive, growth-oriented thoughts. She also encourages readers to challenge themselves and move out of their comfort zones, as this is the best way to grow and develop.

"Mindset: The New Psychology of Success" offers an insightful look at the importance of thinking and beliefs in our lives and accomplishments. By exploring the concept of mindset, Dweck sheds light on the power of self-belief and its influence on our behaviors, choices, and success. This book encourages readers to explore and develop their thinking about their abilities and embrace a growth mindset as the key to success and fulfillment.

Passionate South Africans!

There are several South African writers and thinkers who can offer valuable insights on the theme of passion. Some examples of South African writers and experts that you may want to read up upon are:

Thuli Madonsela: As a South African advocate and professor of legal studies, she has set an example of passion and integrity in her career. She rose to prominence as the Public Protector of South Africa. She built a reputation as a champion for law and justice during her tenure. Her story can be a source of inspiration for people who want to follow their passions in the fight for a just society.

Mamphela Ramphele: Ramphele is a South African academic, politician, and activist who became famous as an advocate for human rights and social justice. She has had a long career in public service and academia. She has contributed to the promotion of democracy and inclusivity in South Africa. Her story can encourage people to follow their passions in pursuing societal change and improvement.

Pieter-Dirk Uys: Uys is a South African satirist, writer, and activist who became famous for his critical commentary on social and political issues in South Africa. He had a very successful career as a writer and actor and made a significant impact through his work. His story can inspire people to follow their passions in the arts and culture sector and to make a difference through creativity and expression.

Fulfilling One's Passion

Fulfilling a person's passion plays a vital role at sociological level. It affects individual and communal dynamics, social relations, and social structures. Here are some ways the fulfillment of passion can have a sociological impact:

Community Building and Collaboration: When individuals pursue their passions and become involved in communal projects that feed their passion, it can lead to close-knit communities and a sense of belonging. This cohesion can lead to greater cooperation and social support within the community.

Social Change and Activism: Fulfilling passion can motivate individuals to engage in social change and activism to live up to their passion-driven beliefs. This can lead to the mobilization of resources and the incentive of others to also engage in social issues and activities.

Economic Impact: Passionate individuals can have a substantial financial impact by creating new business opportunities, innovation, and economic growth. Living out passions can lead to developing new products, services, and enterprises that create jobs and stimulate the economy.

Identity Formation and Self-Expression: Passion plays a role in shaping an individual's identity and self-expression. By following their passions, people can develop a strong sense of self-realization and self-awareness, impacting how they see themselves and get on in the world.

Social Structure and Institutions: The fulfillment of passion can change social structures and institutions by promoting new ideas, values, and norms promoted by passionate individuals and groups. This can lead to the adaptation of social structures to better suit the needs and interests of the community.

In general, fulfilling a person's passion can have a significant sociological impact through promoting community building, social change, economic development, identity formation, and the adaptation of social structures and institutions.

Passion In Business And Society

To describe the influence of living out a person's passion as a success in various contexts such as business, sport, politics, and the humanitarian sphere, a variety of literature and studies explore this topic. This literature and studies focus on the role of passion in achieving excellence, achievement, and success in various domains. Herewith an overview of relevant literature and studies in each context, including statistical data where available.

The Business World

"Good to Great" by Jim Collins: This book explores the characteristics of successful businesses and identifies the concept of "level 5 leadership" as a critical factor for long-term success. This highlights the importance of passion and commitment in leading companies that excel and succeed.

"Drive: The Surprising Truth About What Motivates Us" by Daniel Pink: In this book, Pink explores the factors that drive intrinsic motivation, including the role of passion in achieving success in the work environment. He argues that passion is critical in encouraging self-motivated workers who pursue achievement and success.

"The Lean Startup" by Eric Ries: This book discusses the principles of lean startup methodologies and highlights the importance of passion and iterative development in creating successful startups. It explores the role of passion in encouraging resilience and innovation in the business world.

Sports

"Grit: The Power of Passion and Perseverance" by Angela Duckworth: In this book, Duckworth explores the concept of "grit" and identifies it as a critical factor for success in multiple domains, including sports. She discusses the role of passion and perseverance in achieving excellence and achievement in sport.

"The Inner Game of Tennis" by Timothy Gallwey: This book explores the psychological aspects of sports performance and highlights the importance of passion, focus, and self-awareness in achieving success on the tennis court. It provides insights into the role of passion in improving sports performance.

Politics

"The Audacity of Hope" by Barack Obama: In this book, Obama shares his personal stories and reflections on the role of passion and commitment in his political career. He stressed the importance of a passionate commitment to serving the public in achieving success in the political arena.

"The Education of an Idealist" by Samantha Power: In this memoir, Power describes her experiences as a diplomatic officer and the role of passion in the pursuit of international peace and human rights. She stressed the importance of passion and determination in achieving political and human rights activism success.

Humanitarian levels

"Half the Sky: Turning Oppression into Opportunity for Women Worldwide" by Nicholas Kristof and Sheryl WuDunn: This book explores the challenges women face worldwide and highlights the role of passion and activism in the fight against women's oppression. It provides statistical data and case studies to illustrate the impact of passionate engagement in the humanitarian arena.

"Mountains Beyond Mountains" by Tracy Kidder: This book tells the true story of physician Paul Farmer and his passionate mission to provide health care to people in developing countries. It illustrates the power of passion and commitment in alleviating human suffering and promoting human well-being.

This literature and studies offer insights into the role of passion as a success-determining factor in multiple domains and illustrate its impact on individual achievement and everyday well-being. By integrating statistical data, personal stories, and academic research, these sources provide a comprehensive understanding of the importance of passion in achieving success and excellence.

Simon Sinek And Passion

The "Start with WHY" concept by Simon Sinek is a powerful framework that emphasizes the importance of a clear and deep understanding of your purpose and motivation behind everything you do.

Connect with your Passion: Sinek stresses understanding why you do something before you know how or what. In the context of passion, you can encourage people to connect deeply with the why behind their passions. Why do they passionately feel about a particular activity, calling, or interest? By identifying this "why," people can commit more to their passions.

Inspire Action through Passion: Sinek argues that people are spurred to action when they firmly commit to the purpose or cause behind the action. In the context of passion, you can encourage people to see their passions as a powerful source of motivation and inspiration for action. When people deeply understand the why behind their passions, they will be more likely to take steps to progress in them.

Share Personal Stories and Examples: Sinek emphasizes the power of personal stories and examples to illustrate a message and inspire people.

Direct Practical Exercises: Sinek encourages the reader to do practical exercises to identify and understand their "why."

The Role of Peter Drucker in Living Passion in the World of Work

Peter Drucker, a pioneer in management science and leadership, has made an indelible mark on the business world with his insights and ideas on effective management and organizational performance. Drucker not only influenced management practice techniques but also stressed the importance of passion in the work environment. In this Chapter, we will explore the role of Peter Drucker in living out passion in the world of work and the impact his thinking has had on the modern business world.

The Early Life and Education of Peter Drucker

Before we explore Peter Drucker's influence on living out passion in the world of work, it is crucial to give a brief overview of his early life and education.

Drucker was born Nov. 19, 1909, in Vienna, Austria-Hungary, and devoted his life to academic research and writing. He obtained a doctorate in international law from the University of Frankfurt before starting his career as an author and consultant.

The Contribution of Peter Drucker to Management Science

Peter Drucker is widely regarded as the father of management science, and his contribution to the field is immeasurable. He developed a series of groundbreaking ideas and concepts that are still considered fundamental governance and leadership principles today. Some of Drucker's most famous works include "The Practice of Management" (1954), "The Effective Executive" (1967), and "Innovation and Entrepreneurship" (1985).

Drucker's thinking has changed how people view management and leadership in the business world. He emphasized the importance of effective management, strategic planning, and innovative leadership, and his work laid the foundation for many of the management practices still used today.

The Importance of Passion in the Work Environment

One of the core principles Peter Drucker emphasized was the importance of passion in the work environment. He believed that passion is a critical factor in the success of individuals and organizations and that employees who are passionate about their work are likelier to exhibit high levels of engagement and productivity.

Drucker emphasized that passion is not just an emotional state but a state of sustained energy and commitment to a goal. He believed that passionate employees produce their best work, generate innovative ideas, and have a meaningful impact on their organizations.

Drucker's Ideas on Motivation and Leadership

Peter Drucker contributed significantly to understanding motivation and leadership in the work environment. He believed that effective leadership is vital to fostering passion and engagement among employees, and he stressed the importance of inspiring leaders who have a vision and create a culture of trust and support.

Drucker also stressed the importance of reward and recognition in employee motivation. He believed that employees who receive recognition for their work and are rewarded for their contributions are likelier to be passionate about their work and deliver on their best efforts.

The Influence of Drucker's Thought on the Modern Business World

Peter Drucker's thinking about passion in the work environment has profoundly impacted the modern business world. Many businesses have implemented his ideas on motivation, leadership, and management to foster a culture of passion and engagement among their employees.

Drucker's focus on the importance of passion and engagement has laid the groundwork for many current initiatives in employee engagement and employee relations. Many businesses have focused on creating a positive work environment that encourages passion and engagement.

The Legacy of Peter Drucker

The contribution of Peter Drucker to management science and business as a whole cannot be overstated. His thinking about passion and its importance in the work environment has profoundly impacted how enterprises manage and motivate their employees.

Drucker's heritage lives on in today's management practices and leadership philosophies, and his ideas about passion in the work environment inspire leaders and managers worldwide.

The Role of Passion in the Works of John Maxwell: An In-Depth Investigation

John C. Maxwell is a renowned author, speaker, and leadership expert who has had a considerable impact on the business world and the personal development of individuals. His work focuses on various aspects of leadership, including the importance of passion in the work environment. In this chapter, we will explore the role of passion in the works of John Maxwell, as well as how he implements and encourages passion in a working context.

The Core Principles of John Maxwell's Work

John Maxwell focuses on developing leadership qualities and fostering a positive work environment. His books, including "The 21 Irrefutable Laws of Leadership" and "The 5 Levels of Leadership," provide valuable insights and strategic guidelines for developing effective leadership.

One of the core principles that runs through Maxwell's work is the importance of passion in the work environment. He believes that passion is a critical factor in the success of individuals and organizations and that leadership motivated by a deep passion for the job can profoundly impact employee performance and engagement.

The Implementation of Passion in a Working Context

John Maxwell implements passion in a working context by creating a culture of inspiration and positive energy. He encourages leaders to communicate their passion for the job and create an environment that encourages employees to pursue their passions.

One of the ways Maxwell implements passion in a working context is by promoting a vision that inspires and motivates people. He encourages leaders to create a clear and inspiring vision for the organization and to communicate the importance of this vision with passion.

Maxwell also stresses the importance of a positive and supportive work environment that encourages employees to pursue their passions. He encourages leaders to create a climate of trust and acceptance where employees can be themselves and reach their potential.

Motivated Employers to Encourage Passion in Work

John Maxwell is a big proponent of the importance of leadership motivated by passion and vision. He encourages employers to adopt a passionate approach to leadership and to share their passion for working with employees.

One of the ways Maxwell motivates employers to encourage passion in work is by emphasizing the impact of passionate leadership on employee performance and engagement. He encourages leaders to communicate their passion for the work and to create a culture of inspiration and positive energy.

Maxwell also stresses the importance of a healthy work-life balance that allows employees to pursue their passions outside of work. He encourages employers to give employees the space and support to pursue their out-of-work passions, which can positively impact their overall well-being and productivity.

Encouraging Employees to Live Their Passion

John Maxwell encourages employees to live out their passion by emphasizing the importance of self-awareness and self-discovery. He encourages employees to identify their inner passions and to take steps to pursue these passions, even within the work environment.

One of the ways Maxwell encourages employees to live out their passion is by creating a culture of self-development and growth. He encourages employees to develop through continuous learning and personal development, which can help them identify and pursue their passions.

Maxwell also encourages employees to take a proactive approach to their career development and actively look for opportunities to fulfill their passions. He encourages employees to make their voices heard and to share their ideas and passions with their employers, which can lead to opportunities for growth and development.

The Heritage of John Maxwell's Work

The work of John Maxwell has had a profound impact on the business world and the personal development of individuals worldwide. His focus on the importance of passion in the world of work has considerably impacted how leadership and management are approached in the modern business world.

Maxwell's books and speakership have become a source of inspiration for many who strive for a meaningful and successful work environment. His work has left a legacy of passion and inspiration that will continue for decades.

Conclusion

The role of passion in the works of John Maxwell is a core aspect of his contribution to the field of leadership and management science.

The Role of Passion in the Business World: An Analysis of "Good to Great" by Jim Collins

The business world is a dynamic and competitive environment where businesses strive for excellence and success. In his book "Good to Great: Why Some Companies Make the Leap... and Others Don't," Jim Collins takes leaders to examine the characteristics of exceptional businesses and understand what sets them apart. One of the core concepts Collins emphasizes is the role of passion in a company's success.

This chapter will focus on the concept of passion outlined by Collins and how it is a critical factor for transforming from good businesses to large enterprises.

The Essence of "Good to Great"

"Good to Great" is a bestselling book based on pioneering research and offers an in-depth analysis of what sets the best companies apart. Collins and his team undertook a five-year study to identify companies that had achieved long-term excellence. They summarized their findings in this book. The book identifies the key characteristics of these "large" companies. It examines the leadership and business practices that have made them successful.

One of the study's striking findings was that not only did the best companies have excellent management practices and strategic decisions, but they also demonstrated a deep-rooted passion for their work and goals. Collins clarifies: "The greatest leaders have had not only a passion for what they do but also a passion for the people they do it with and the clients they serve."

The Concept of Passion in the Business World

According to Collins, passion is essential for transforming from an excellent company to a big one. He describes passion as a deep-rooted belief in the purpose and mission of the company and an unstoppable desire to achieve excellence. It goes beyond an emotional state; It is a powerful driving force that motivates leaders and teams to give their best and strive for greatness.

According to Collins, the leaders of large companies are passionate individuals who demonstrate a profound commitment to their work and goals. These leaders transfer their passion to their teams by creating an inspiring vision and cultivating an environment of enthusiasm and dedication. The result is a culture of excellence and achievement that enables the company to achieve its goals and maintain long-term success.

The Effects of Passion on Business Performance

The impact of passion on business performance is considerable and is identified by Collins as a critical factor for success. When leaders and teams are passionate about their work, they display higher engagement, commitment, and creativity. This passion leads to improved work, a greater willingness to accept challenges, and an increased ability to find successful solutions to problems.

In addition, passion fosters an environment of cooperation and cooperation within the company. When individuals share their passion and work together toward a common goal, they create a culture of trust, respect, and support that promotes the company's performance and success.

Statistical data and supporting research

Research and statistics support the link between passion and business performance. A study by Gallup found that companies with higher levels of employee engagement, often associated with passion, show a higher level of productivity, profitability, and customer pride. In addition, there is a strong positive correlation between the passion of management and employees and the company's overall performance.

The Role of Passion in Practice

Collins' work has had a profound impact on the business world. It has encouraged leaders and companies to recognize passion as a critical component of their business strategies. Many companies have integrated passion into their culture and management practices and have intensely focused on fostering an environment where passion can thrive.

In today's business world, recognizing the importance of passion as a success-determining factor is essential to achieving excellence and sustainability. By cultivating and nurturing passion, companies can create a culture of inspiration, commitment, and achievement that enables them to excel and positively impact their industry and the world.

Concluding Thoughts

"Good to Great" by Jim Collins offers an insightful look at the role of passion in transforming good businesses into big business. By emphasizing the importance of passion and commitment in business, Collins contributes to a deeper understanding of how companies can be successful and maintain long-term excellence. His work inspires firms and leaders to embrace and use their passion as a powerful driver of success.

The Role of Steven Covey in Living Passion in the Workplace

Steven Covey was an influential author, speaker, and leadership expert who became famous for his personal and professional development work. His books, including "The 7 Habits of Highly Effective People," have inspired and influenced millions worldwide.

In this Chapter, we will explore Covey's role in living out an employer and employee's fulfillment of passion and how his thinking impacted workplace culture and leadership practices.

The Philosophy of Steven Covey

Steven Covey advocated for a holistic approach to leadership and personal development. His philosophy was based on the belief that true success should be aimed at external achievements, inner fulfillment, and integrity. He identified various principles and habits that guide effective leadership and personal growth.

One of the principles Covey emphasized was the importance of identifying and living out an individual's passion in the workplace.

He believed that passion is at the heart of motivation and success and that when employers and employees can identify and pursue their passion, it leads to higher engagement, productivity, and satisfaction.

Living Passion in the Workplace

For Covey, living out passion in the workplace has been essential to a successful and fulfilled career. He believed that when employees can pursue their passion in their work, it leads to a sense of purpose and meaning, positively impacting their overall performance.

Creating an environment that fosters passion has been a critical responsibility for employers. Covey believed employers should create a supportive and encouraging culture where employees could express and develop their passion. This includes identifying individual strengths and interests, promoting self-leadership, and creating opportunities for personal growth and development.

The Impact on the Workplace Culture

Steven Covey's thinking has had a noticeable impact on workplace culture worldwide. Many companies have integrated effective leadership and personal development principles into their business practices. This has led to a shift towards a more people-oriented approach to leadership, with a strong focus on recognizing individual employees' unique needs and interests.

Employers who have integrated the principles of Covey into their business practices have often created an environment that fosters and encourages passion. These companies experienced higher employee engagement and satisfaction, directly impacting their overall performance and success.

The Application in Practice

In practice, Covey's philosophy led to an increased awareness and attention to the needs and interests of individual employees. Employers have begun to create more flexible and adaptable work environments that accommodate the diversity of passions and interests of their employees.

This approach has resulted in higher employee engagement, productivity, and satisfaction. It also contributed to a culture of trust, respect, and cooperation, improving the overall work climate and fostering the company's success.

Conclusion

Steven Covey has indelibly impacted workplace culture and leadership practices by emphasizing the importance of passion in living out an employer and employee fulfillment. His philosophy has created a greater awareness and appreciation of the role of passion in the work environment. It has led to a shift towards a more people-oriented and supportive approach to leadership. By embracing its principles, companies have had the opportunity to create a culture that fosters and encourages passion, which has directly impacted their overall performance and success.

The Role of Passion in the Maintenance and Realization of Maslow's Pyramid of Need

Abraham Maslow's pyramid of needs, also known as the hierarchy of needs, is a world-renowned theory that hierarchically arranges human needs. The pyramid consists of five levels of needs, starting with basic physiological needs and ending with self-realization. In this Chapter, we will explore the role of passion in maintaining and realizing Maslow's pyramid and how living out passion contributes to fulfilling various needs at each level of the pyramid.

The Basic Concept of Maslow's Need Pyramid

Maslow's pyramid of needs is a model that hierarchically organizes human needs. It starts with physiological needs such as food, water, and shelter, followed by safety, social needs, recognition, and self-realization. The theory suggests that people will focus on a lower level of the pyramid before moving on to a higher level.

The Connection Between Passion and Maslow's Need Pyramid

Passion plays an essential role in fulfilling needs at every level of Maslow's pyramid. Here's how passion contributes to maintaining and realizing the needs at every level:

Physiological needs:

Living out passion can directly impact the fulfillment of physiological needs. Passion can motivate people to promote their physical health, such as maintaining an active lifestyle and following healthy eating habits to nourish and care for their bodies.

Safety Needs:

Living out passion can also promote a sense of safety and security. When people are passionate about their work or life purpose, it creates a sense of stability and self-confidence that enables them to ensure their future safety through financial planning and career development.

Social Needs:

Passion can play a critical role in fostering social connections and relationships. Sharing their passions with others creates a sense of community and cooperation that contributes to fulfilling social needs such as love, acceptance, and connectedness.

Acknowledgement:

Living out passion can foster a sense of recognition and accomplishment. When people pursue their passions and achieve their goals, they often receive recognition and praise for their achievements, satisfying an essential need for recognition and self-appreciation.

5. Self-realization:

Ultimately, passion can play a critical role in achieving self-realization. Passion is the force that motivates people to reach their full potential, develop their talents and skills, and pursue their dreams. Living out passion leads to a sense of satisfaction and fulfillment, representing the culmination of Maslow's pyramid.

Practical Examples and Studies

Several studies and examples illustrate the relationship between passion and the fulfillment of needs outlined in Maslow's pyramid of needs. For example:

- A research study by Csikszentmihalyi (1990) found that people who occupy themselves with activities in which they are passionate often experience a state of "flow," which is characterized by a high level of concentration and fulfillment.
- In another study by Deci and Ryan (2000), it was found that people who occupy themselves with activities that intrinsically motivate them, such as passionate interests, experience a higher level of self-realization and well-being.

In the context of Maslow's pyramid of needs, passion plays a critical role in maintaining and realizing human needs. Living out passion fulfills physiological, safety, social, recognition, and self-realization needs. This link between passion and the fulfillment of needs has been underpinned by research and practical examples. It emphasizes the importance of living passion for a fulfilled and meaningful life.

Further Sources to consult:

- Csikszentmihalyi, M. (1990). Flow: The psychology of optimal experience. Harper & Row.
- Deci, E. L., & Ryan, R. M. (2000). The" what" and" why" of goal pursuits: Human needs and the self-determination of behavior. Psychological Inquiry, 11(4), 227-268.

Kobus Neethling And Passion

Kobus Neethling is a well-known South African author and motivational speaker specializing in emotional intelligence, creativity, and passion.

The Psychology of Passion: Neethling has written extensively on the psychology of passion and has developed several theories and models to understand and cultivate passion.

The Nature of Passion

Passion can be described as a solid and persistent emotional state that involves a deep longing or interest in a particular activity, purpose, or interest. This is often accompanied by intense feelings and a strong sense of engagement and fulfillment.

The nature of passion can vary from individual to individual.

It can take various forms, including personal passions such as creativity, sport, and knowledge and professional passions such as career development and social impact.

The Psychological Underlying Principles of Passion

The psychological underlying principles of passion are complex and influenced by various factors. One of the fundamental principles is the concept of intrinsic motivation, which refers to the drive to complete a task or achieve a goal because of the inner joy and fulfillment it provides. People with strong intrinsic motivation for a particular activity or interest are often more likely to perceive it as a passion.

Another essential principle is the concept of self-determination, which refers to the sense of choice and control over our behavior and circumstances. When people experience a sense of self-determination in pursuing their passions, they often feel more motivated and involved.

The Role of Emotions and Motivation

Emotions play a critical role in the emergence and sustainment of passion. Positive emotions such as excitement, joy, and enthusiasm can be a strong motivating force behind pursuing passions. On the other hand, negative emotions such as frustration, discouragement, and disappointment can interfere with the ability to follow passions.

Motivation is also an essential factor in the development of passion. External motivation, such as rewards or praise from others, can have a short-lived influence on our behavior. Still, the inner joy and self-realization that result from intrinsic motivation often lead to sustainable passion.

Discovering and Checking Passions

Discovering and checking passions is a personal and unique process for each individual. It can start with self-reflection and introspection, which helps people identify what they feel genuinely passionate about. In addition, experimentation with various activities and interests can help discover new passions and develop a deeper understanding of existing passions.

People can also further check their passions by developing their skills and talent in those areas, seeking mentorship from others who share them, and participating in community initiatives or projects related to them.

The Psychology of Passion in Practice

In practice, the psychology of passion can be applied by helping individuals follow their passions and build a life based on the things they love most. This can include identifying career possibilities that align with their passions, cultivating an environment that supports them, and establishing realistic goals and expectations for their passion projects.

In addition, the psychology of passion can also be applied to promoting a healthy work-life balance, dealing with stress and burnout, and promoting self-care and well-being while people pursue their passions.

In this extensive Chapter, an overview of the various aspects of the psychology of passion is provided, including its nature, the psychological underlying principles, the role of emotions and motivation, and how people can discover and check their passions. By developing a deeper understanding of these concepts, individuals can better understand and pursue their passions, thus leading a more fulfilling and meaningful life.

Practical Exercises and Tools: Neethling has developed several practical exercises and tools to help people identify and develop their passions.

Self-reflection exercises

Self-reflection is a critical aspect of the process of discovering and understanding passions. It allows individuals to dwell on their interests, preferences, values, and goals. Various self-reflection exercises can be used to develop a deeper understanding of personal passions:

Living wheel: The living wheel is a self-reflection exercise that helps people assess the different aspects of their lives, including career, family, friends, health, creativity, and more. By grading each area according to your satisfaction, you can identify which areas of your life you want to pay more attention to and where your passions lie.

Passion board: A passion board is a creative exercise in which you visually represent your dreams, goals, and passions. It may consist of photos, quotes, word quotes, and other objects that represent your passions and inspirations. It is a constant reminder of what you are passionate about and want to achieve.

Career tracking questionnaire: A career tracking questionnaire is a valuable tool for identifying an individual's passions and preferences in terms of career. This questionnaire may include questions about personal interests, skills, values, and what gives a person fulfillment and meaning in their work.

Creative discovery activities

Creative discovery activities offer a practical and hands-on approach to discovering passions. These activities can help individuals learn new interests and cultivate their existing passions:

Artistic Expression: Encourage individuals to explore various artistic mediums, such as painting, drawing, writing, music making, sculpting, and more. These creative forms of expression can allow individuals to explore and express their emotions, expressions, and passions.

Nature tracking: Encourage individuals to spend time in nature and try hiking, biking, kayaking, and astronomical observation. Nature tracking can foster a sense of peace, wonder, and connections to nature, which in turn can encourage the discovery of personal passions.

Trial Experience Learning Experiences: Encouraging individuals to participate in trial experience learning experiences, such as workshops, courses, and seminars in various areas of interest. These learning experiences allow individuals to develop new skills, discover new interests, and better understand their passions.

Objective scoring and evaluating

After identifying and exploring potential passions, setting goals and evaluating progress is essential. These steps can help individuals develop a practical plan for pursuing their passions and staying motivated and focused:

SMART Goals: Encourage individuals to set specific, measurable, achievable, relevant, and time-proof goals for their passions. These goals can serve as a signpost for the actions and initiatives to be taken to follow their passions.

Self-Evaluation: Encourage individuals to regularly review and evaluate their progress. This can provide an opportunity for self-reflection on what works, what doesn't, and what needs to be adjusted to pursue their passions.

Adaptation and Growth: Remind individuals that discovering and following their passions is an ongoing journey that requires adjustment and growth. Encourage them to be open to change and new opportunities that may arise and to keep learning and growing in the process.

In general, practical exercises and tools can play a valuable role in discovering, developing, and exercising passions. These exercises provide a structured framework for individuals to identify, experiment, and cultivate their passions. They can be a critical step in achieving a fulfilling and meaningful life.

Passion in Different Contexts: Neethling also wrote about how passion appears in different contexts, including the workplace, school environment, and personal life.

Passion manifests in different contexts, including personal, professional, cultural, and social. Each context offers a unique opportunity for individuals to discover, cultivate, and live out their passions. I will further explore the different contexts of passion and how it can impact and improve individuals' lives.

Personal context

In the personal context, passion is often attached to individual interests, goals, and values. This can include various areas of interest, such as creative expressions (such as art, music, and writing), sports and health activities, travel and adventure, and personal growth and development. Expressing passion in the personal context provides an opportunity for self-expression, self-realization, and joy.

Individuals can discover their passions in the personal context through self-reflection, experimentation with various activities, and participation in community and cultural events.

For example, someone passionate about travel may participate in local travel groupings, attend travel-related workshops, or even start travel blogs to share their adventures with others.

Professional context

In the professional context, passion often refers to a deep sense of involvement and commitment to a particular career or profession. This can be a significant driver of success and fulfillment in the workplace.

People who pursue their passions professionally are often more likely to be creative and innovative, develop their skills, and make a positive impact in their careers.

Individuals can develop their passions in the professional context by focusing on career areas aligned with their interests and skills, seeking mentorship from experienced craftspeople in their field, and participating in professional development opportunities that expand their knowledge and skills.

For example, a person passionate about the environment might pursue a career in environmental conservation or green technologies.

Cultural context

In the cultural context, passion can be attached to an individual's cultural identity, heritage, and community. This may mean that people are passionate about preserving their cultural heritage, promoting social justice for their communities, or participating in cultural activities and celebrations important to their identities.

Individuals can pursue their passions in the cultural context by participating in cultural events, organizations, and activities that celebrate and promote their cultural heritage. For example, a person passionate about preserving indigenous culture may become involved in local cultural associations or community projects promoting the preservation of traditional knowledge and practices.

Social context

In the social context, passion refers to a deep engagement with and commitment to social causes and activism. This may mean humans are passionate about advancing social justice, protecting human and animal rights, or promoting peace and tolerance.

Individuals can develop their passions in the social context by participating in social movements, organizations, and activities that reflect their beliefs and values. For example, a person passionate about promoting social justice might get involved with local community organizations, participate in peace protests, or even start their own social movement.

The Connection of Different Contexts

While each context of passion presents unique opportunities and challenges, it is crucial to recognize that these contexts are not always separate, and there is often overlap between them. For example, a person's personal passions may influence their career choices and social engagement. In contrast, their professional passions may shape their personal lives and cultural identity. Exploring passion in different contexts can help people develop a more holistic approach to discovering, cultivating, and living out their passions.

The Significant Impact of Passion in Different Contexts

The expression of passion in different contexts can significantly impact the lives of individuals and the societies in which they participate. Personal passions can be a source of joy, fulfillment, and self-identification. In contrast, professional passions can lead to career success and personal growth. Cultural and societal passions can impact communities and the world by promoting cultural preservation, social justice, and positive change.

Overall, expressing passion in different contexts can play a critical role in the lives of individuals and the societies in which they live. It provides an opportunity for self-expression, self-realization, and positive impact, and it can be a significant source of joy, meaning, and fulfillment in life.

Motivational practices: As a motivational speaker, Neethling also has valuable insights on motivating people to follow their passions and reach their full potential

The concept of motivation plays a crucial role in the discovery, development, and exercise of passions. Motivational practices are strategies and techniques individuals can use to motivate themselves, stay focused, and follow their passions. I will explore a variety of motivational practices and how they can positively influence the expression of passion.

Self-reflection and goal-scoring

Self-reflection is a critical starting point for the development of motivation. By looking back at personal values, goals, and passions, an individual can better understand themselves and form a clearer picture of what they want to achieve. This self-reflection can be complemented by setting goals that are specific, measurable, achievable, relevant, and time-bound (SMART). These goals create a signpost for the individual and help develop a sense of purpose and focus.

Visualizations and Affirmations

Visualization and affirmations are powerful techniques that can be used to cultivate motivation and build confidence. Creating a clear picture of what an individual wants to achieve and visualizing it repeatedly can help create a strong and positive image of the future. Affirmations, or positive self-talk, can also play an essential role in building self-confidence and self-belief. By repeatedly making positive self-statements, individuals can motivate themselves and strengthen their abilities to achieve their goals.

Positive Thinking and Mindset

A positive thinking and growth mindset can be a powerful motivational force for individuals pursuing their passions. A growth mindset involves the belief that intelligence, skills, and talent can be developed through hard work, dedication, and perseverance. These ways of thinking can help individuals see their challenges as opportunities for growth and motivate themselves to persevere, even in the face of trouble.

Rewards and Positive Reinforcements

Rewards and positive reinforcements can be an effective way to cultivate and maintain motivation. By implementing a reward system that rewards achieving goals and exercising passions, individuals can be motivated to move on and persevere. This can take several forms, including physical rewards, such as a particular treatment or a reward trip, or emotional rewards, such as praise and recognition from others.

Peer Support and Mentorship

Peer support and mentoring are critical motivational practices that help individuals develop and sustain their passions. By participating in supportive communities, such as groups or clubs with common interests, individuals can get encouragement and support from like-minded individuals. Mentoring provides a unique opportunity for individuals to learn from experienced individuals who have already pursued their passions and to get guidance on how to succeed in those areas.

Accountability and Self-Management

Accountability and self-management are critical motivational practices that help individuals achieve their passions. By having some responsibility for their actions and progressions, individuals can be motivated to set and pursue goals. Self-management involves the ability to determine for yourself the direction of your life, including identifying passions and taking action to achieve them. It requires self-awareness, discipline, and commitment but can be a powerful tool for self-motivation and success.

In general, motivational practices provide a framework and techniques for individuals to motivate themselves, stay focused, and follow their passions. By implementing these practices, individuals can develop a strong and sustainable motivation that helps them succeed in pursuing their passions and goals.

The Power of Self-Discovery: An Analysis of "Let Your Life Speak" by Parker Palmer

"Let Your Life Speak" by Parker J. Palmer is an influential book exploring self-discovery and self-realization. In this Chapter, we will explore the fundamental concepts of the book as well as the impact they have had on readers' understanding of self-knowledge and vocation.

The Essence of "Let Your Life Speak"

"Let Your Life Speak" is a work that offers a profound insight into self-discovery and self-realization. Parker Palmer shares personal experiences and insights as he guides the reader to find and follow the inner voice that calls for a fulfilled and meaningful life.

The book's title, "Let Your Life Speak," refers to the idea that our lives have a message to share with the world and that our true calling is found by listening to the silence of our hearts and following the unique path meant for us.

Key concepts and themes

Self-discovery: One of the book's central themes is the importance of self-discovery. Palmer emphasizes the need to pause, look inward, and discover the true self amidst the noise of the world around us.

Calling: "Let Your Life Speak" explores calling as an inner call to make a unique contribution to the world. Palmer encourages readers to embrace their true calling and to stay true to their unique gifts and passions.

Integrity: Palmer stresses the importance of integrity in life and career. He argues that to find our life purpose, we must live in alignment with our inner truths and values.

Determination: The book encourages lifelong learning and growth, emphasizing the importance of determination and persistence in pursuing self-realization.

The Impact on Readers

"Let Your Life Speak" has had a meaningful impact on readers by inspiring them to develop a deeper understanding of themselves and follow their calling. Readers praised the book for its honesty, sincerity, and deep insights into the human experience.

Many readers said that the book helped them to get a brighter picture of themselves and to find the courage to follow their true calling. This led to fulfillment and meaning in their lives and careers.

Concluding Thoughts

"Let Your Life Speak" by Parker J. Palmer is an exceptional work exploring self-discovery and self-realization. By sharing honest personal experiences and guiding the reader to find and follow the inner voice, Palmer has profoundly impacted readers' understanding of self-knowledge and calling. The book remains a source of inspiration for those looking for a deeper understanding of themselves and their place in the world.

Sources To Consult

- Palmer, P. J. (2000). Let Your Life Speak: Listening for the Voice of Vocation. Jossey-Bass.

The Meaning of In-Between: An Examination of "The In-Between" by Hadley Vlahos

Hadley Vlahos' book, "The In-Between," offers an intimate look at the human experience of life between life and death. In this article, we will explore the fundamental concepts of the book, as well as the influence of Vlahos' role at the hospice in the writing process.

The Essence of "The In-Between"

"The In-Between" is a moving exploration of the in-between phase of human life, focusing on the experiences of people moving to a hospice. Vlahos paints a moving picture of the human experience of saying goodbye and the uncertainties of life after the diagnosis of a life-shortening disease.

The book offers an honest and uncovered look at the emotional, physical, and spiritual challenges of living in a hospice. Still, it never loses the hope, humanity, and dignity of those who live through those last stages of life.

Key concepts and themes

Farewell and Loss: One of the book's main themes is the theme of parting and loss. Vlahos poignantly describes the emotional journey of those confronted with the reality of a life-shortening illness, as well as its impact on their loved ones.

Acceptance and Peace: "The In-Between" also explores the process of acceptance and the search for peace amidst life's challenges between life and death. Vlahos paints a picture of the inner struggle and eventual acceptance that often occurs in patients in a hospice.

Humanity and Dignity: A central theme in the book is preserving humanity and dignity in difficult circumstances. Vlahos stressed the importance of loving care and respect for the human experience in the final stages of life.

The Influence of Vlahos' Role at the Hospice

The influence of Vlahos' role at the hospice is visible throughout the pages of "The In-Between."

As a nurse at the hospice, Vlahos got an intimate look at the human experience of life and death, and these experiences formed the foundation for her book.

Her work at the hospice allowed her to share deeply personal stories and give a voice to the people living through the final stages of their lives.

These experiences allowed her to cast an honest and unexposed look at the human experience of life and death. They helped her capture the emotional depth and humanity of her book.

The Impact of "The In-Between"

"The In-Between" has had a meaningful impact on readers by encouraging them to view the human experience of life and death with a new lens. The book offers an intimate and moving look at the human spirit and the power of love, acceptance, and hope, even amid the darkest times.

Readers praised the book for its sincerity, fellow humanity, and deep personal insight. It served as a reminder of the value of every moment and the importance of loving care and empathy in the final stages of life.

Conclusion

"The In-Between" by Hadley Vlahos offers a moving and intimate look at the human experience of life and death. With a deep understanding of the human spirit and an intimate look at life between life and death, Vlahos' book made an indelible impression on readers worldwide. It serves as a reminder of the value of every moment and the power of love, acceptance, and hope amid the darkest times.

Sources to Consult

- Vlahos, H. (2020). The In-Between. HarperCollins.

Jim Collins And Passion

Jim Collins is an influential author and management consultant known for his work on business management and leadership. His books, such as "Good to Great" and "Built to Last," have profoundly impacted the business and management world, but their impact extends beyond that. Collins' insights have also contributed to understanding and expressing passion personally and professionally.

One of the main ways Jim Collins has influenced my passion is by emphasizing the importance of purposefulness and commitment to excellence. In his books, he discusses the concept of "a Hedgehog concept," which involves the idea that successful organizations (and individuals) should clearly understand what they do best, what they are passionate about, and what is economically viable. This concept has helped me identify my passions and focus on the areas where I can make the greatest impact and be most satisfied.

Furthermore, Collins' approach to business leadership and organizational excellence inspired me to live out my passion through the constant pursuit of growth and improvement. He stressed the importance of modest leadership, a commitment to developing talent and focusing on long-term success. These principles have led me to create an environment where I can express my passions by empowering others to reach their potential and continually grow and improve.

In his books and recitals, Collins shares personal stories of success and failure, which helped me understand the reality of pursuing my passions. He stressed the importance of resilience and perseverance in the face of challenges and failures, which encouraged me not to get too discouraged but to see every experience as an opportunity for growth and learning.

In short, the work of Jim Collins has helped me identify, focus, and pursue my passions in a way that not only brings personal fulfillment but also impacts the world around me. Through his insights into purposefulness, dedication, and perseverance, Collins inspired me to follow my passions and be my best self in everything I do.

Dr. Myles Munroe And Passion

Dr. Myles Munroe, a well-known preacher, author, and motivational speaker, has played a crucial role in promoting self-discovery and self-development, including identifying passion as a driving force in individuals. Although Munroe is not directly known for his work on the concept of passion like other self-help writers, he has promoted a holistic approach to personal development and goal realization that is strongly associated with identifying and expressing passion.

One of Munroe's most important contributions to the concept of passion is his focus on the uniqueness of each individual and the importance of self-discovery. He emphasizes that each person has unique gifts, talents, and passions that set them apart. Through self-discovery and identifying these exceptional qualities, a person can uncover their true potential and find their calling in life.

Munroe encourages people to pursue their passions and choose careers and life paths that align with their gifts and interests. He believes people can lead more fulfilled and purposeful lives following their passions. His insights inspired people to reflect on their passion and take steps to follow those passions.

Furthermore, Munroe's teaching about life goals and destiny impacted the concept of passion. He encourages people to identify their life goals and focus on achieving them with passion and perseverance. He believes that when people pursue their life goals with a fierce passion, they can reach their full potential and impact the world around them.

Although Munroe's work is not explicitly about passion, his holistic approach to self-discovery, life goals, and destiny has played a crucial role in encouraging people to identify and pursue their passions. His inspirational messages and practical tips have guided people to develop a deeper understanding of themselves and to live a life aligned with their true calling and passions.

What If Money Didn't Matter?

The short video titled "What if money didn't matter" is an inspiring and reflective piece that offers a valuable lesson about living out your passion and the importance of personal fulfillment over material rewards. Here are some lessons we can learn from this video:

The Importance of Passion: The video highlights that the money we earn is not the only or even the most crucial measure of success or fulfillment. It focuses on the importance of living out your passion and doing something you are passionate about that makes your soul glow. It reminds us that we find happiness and satisfaction in the things we love and believe in.

The power of purposefulness: The video encourages viewers to think about what they want to do and are passionate about. It stresses the importance of a clear purpose or calling and the continued pursuit of it, even if it does not bring immediate financial rewards. It reminds us that pursuing our passions and goals can give us the deepest fulfillment and meaning in life.

The value of self-discovery: The video encourages self-discovery and the question of what is truly important to each individual. It reminds us that living out our passions is not just about what others expect of us but rather about what we value ourselves and assign ourselves to achieve.

The impact of risk and resilience: The video encourages viewers to take the risk of chasing their passions and not be afraid of failure. It reminds us that the path to success and fulfillment is not always easy but that accepting challenges and continuing to pursue our goals can lead us toward significant growth and fulfillment.

In short, the video "What if money didn't matter" offers a powerful lesson about living out your passion and pursuing purposeful fulfillment in life. It reminds us that true happiness and satisfaction do not always come from external rewards but rather from doing something we are passionate about and believe in.

Determining Your Passion

To gauge a person's passion, various questions and models can be used that help dive deep into the individual's interests, values, and motivational factors. Here are some examples of questions and models that might be helpful:

The Question Model:

- What are the activities or things that make your soul glow?
- What will you volunteer to spend time and energy on without getting paid?
- What goals or projects have aroused your excitement and enthusiasm in the past?

The flame and the fuel model:

- What is deep inside you that ignites your passion (the flame)?
- What feeds this passion and keeps it burning (the fuel)?

The three circuits model:

- What things can you do very well and give you energy (inner circle)?
- What are the things you can do well but not necessarily your passion (middle circle)?
- What are the things that you do poorly and that extract your energy (outside circle)?

The 5 Why Me's?

- Why do you want to achieve this particular goal?
- Why is this goal important to you?
- Why does this goal give you fulfillment or meaning?

- Why do you feel so passionate about this goal?
- Why is this your passion?

These models and questions can help gain a deeper understanding of a person's passions by uncovering their intrinsic motivational factors, values, and interests. It is essential to have an open and respectful conversation with the individual to understand their unique passions and goals as they will form the foundation for their personal growth and fulfillment.

Here is a more detailed extension of the models mentioned above:

The Question Model:

This model focuses on identifying activities and experiences that fuel a person's passion and make their soul glow. The goal is to dive deep into the individual's interests and emotional connections to understand what motivates and fulfills them.

- **What are the activities or things that make your soul glow?** This question examines the individual's emotional responses to specific activities or experiences. These include creative challenges, leadership opportunities, or particular interest interactions.

- **What will you volunteer to spend time and energy on without getting paid?** Asking about what a person will do without any external reward can help determine what they are passionate about and what is intrinsically motivating.

- **What goals or projects have aroused your excitement and enthusiasm in the past?** This question focuses on past experiences that sparked the individual's passion and excitement. This can help identify trends and themes deeply connected to their passions and interests.

The flame and the fuel model:

This model explores the roots and persistent factors that ignite and nourish a person's passion. It focuses on the most profound motivational factors and emotional connections that support and fuel the individual's passions.

- **What is deep inside you that ignites your passion (the flame)?** This question is designed to identify the intrinsic motivational factors that ignite a person's passion. These can be a robust value system, a deep personal interest, or a strong emotional commitment to a specific goal.

- **What feeds this passion and keeps it burning (the fuel)?** Asking about the factors that feed the persistent passion and enthusiasm can help identify the external and internal factors that contribute to the sustained expression of the passion. These can be supportive community relationships, opportunities for growth and development, or a strong internal belief in purpose or goal.

The Three Circles Model:

This model explores the overlap between what a person can do well, what they are passionate about, and what energizes them. It helps to get a holistic picture of areas where a person can live out their passions and reach their full potential.

- **What things can you do very well and give you energy (inner circle)?** This question identifies the areas in which a person has a robust skill set and which provides them with energy when using these skills. It can identify potential opportunities for passionate expression based on a person's skills and strengths.
- **What are the things you can do well but not necessarily your passion (middle circle)?** Identifying what a person can do well but isn't necessarily passionate about can help them understand the limits of their passions and distinguish between what they need to do and want to do.
- **What are the things that you do poorly and that extract your energy (outside circle)?** This question focuses on the areas in which a person has poor skills and which extract their energy when they need to use these skills. This can help identify where to seek help or get support so they can focus on the areas they are passionate about and where they can do their best work.

The Psychology Of Passion

The psychological underlying principles of passion provide a deeper insight into the human experience of passion and how it relates to our emotions, cognition, and behavior. Passion is a complex and subjective emotion that profoundly impacts our well-being and performance in various areas of life, including work, school, personal relationships, and activities. This Chapter will take a closer look at the psychological underlying principles of passion, including the role of emotions, motivation, self-concept, and social influences.

Emotional Dimensions of Passion

Emotions play a crucial role in the experience of passion. Passion is often associated with a strong sense of emotional engagement and excitement in our activities. Several emotional dimensions can be involved in the experience of passion, including:

- **Positive emotions:** Passion can be associated with many positive emotions, such as enthusiasm, excitement, joy, and euphoria. These emotions are a source of energy and motivation for living our passions.

- **Negative emotions:** Although passion is often associated with positive emotions, it can also cause negative emotions, such as anxiety, frustration, and discouragement. These emotions can arise from the challenges and obstacles often associated with pursuing our passions.

- **Emotional intensity:** Passion can be characterized by a high degree of emotional intensity, which allows us to connect with our goals on a deeper level. This emotional intensity can lead to a sense of purpose and focus in our activities.

- **Emotional Change:** Passion can change our emotional state and help us improve our state of mind. For example, living out our passions can bring a sense of accomplishment and joy, while suppressing our desires can lead to emptiness and dissatisfaction.

Motivational Factors of Passion

Motivation plays a vital role in the emergence and sustainable expression of passion. Several factors can play a role in the motivation behind our passions, including:

- **Intrinsic motivation:** Passion is often driven by intrinsic motivation, meaning we are inspired and motivated by activities rather than external rewards. This intrinsic motivation can stem from a deeply personal interest or love for the activities we do.
- **Purposefulness:** Passion is often linked to a strong sense of purpose and meaning. Pursuing our passions provides a sense of purpose and direction, motivating us to work hard and accept challenges to achieve our goals.
- **Flow Experience:** Flow is a state of complete absorption and engagement in an activity, often associated with passionate experiences. When we are in a state of flow, we feel motivated, purposeful, and fulfilled by our activities.
- **Self-appreciation:** Passion is also often linked to positive self-appreciation and self-esteem. Living our passions can strengthen our confidence and self-awareness, motivating us to continue and succeed in our ventures.

Self-concept and passion

Self-concept plays an essential role in the emergence and living out of passion. Our self-concept, or how we see and value ourselves, influences our perceptions of what is important and meaningful to us. Several aspects of self-concept can have an influence on our passions, including:

- **Self-identification:** How we identify ourselves with specific activities or identities can play a role in our passionate engagement with those activities. When we see ourselves as part of any particular community or identity tied to a specific activity, we are more likely to be passionately involved in that activity.
- **Self-Availability:** The extent to which we make ourselves available to live out our passions may be influenced by our self-concept. A strong self-concept and self-confidence can motivate us to take risks and take on challenges to pursue our passions.
- **Self-actualization:** Passion is often tied to the pursuit of self-actualization, meaning we strive for our full potential and purposeful growth and development. A positive self-concept can motivate us to grow and develop towards our passions and to succeed in our undertakings.

Social Influences on Passion

Social factors can have a significant influence on the emergence and sustainable living of passion.

The Role Social Influences Play On Passion

Social influences play a crucial role in developing, forming, and expressing passion. Our social environment, including our family, friends, mentors, and community, significantly impacts the development of our passions and our ability to live them. These influences can be direct or indirect, shaping our values, interests, and motivational factors.

Family and Education

Our family and upbringing play a primary role in shaping our passions. From a young age, we are exposed to various activities and experiences by our parents and family, and this early exposure can profoundly impact our later interests and passions. For example, if a child is exposed to music by their parents, they may develop a passion for music. How our parents support and encourage our interests and passions can significantly impact our self-confidence and our ability to pursue our passions.

In addition, the values and beliefs modelled in our family can also influence our perceptions of what is essential and meaningful. Suppose our parents value a particular career or activity. In that case, it can encourage us to develop our interests. On the other hand, encouraging parents to have a broad range of interests and activities can help us grow and explore a wide range of passions.

Friends and Peer Group

Our friends and peer groups play an essential role in shaping our passions through the social dynamics and group influences they provide. Our tendency is to compare ourselves with our friends and identify ourselves with our peer group's interests and activities. Suppose a friend group is intensely interested in a particular activity. In that case, it can encourage us to participate and develop a passion for that activity.

In addition, our friends can provide a supportive and encouraging environment for living out our passions. When our friends support and encourage our interests and goals, we feel motivated and strengthened to move on and pursue our passions. Our friends can also be a source of inspiration and encouragement by sharing their own passions and successes.

Mentors and role models

Through their influence and guidance, mentors and role models are critical in shaping our passions. Mentors are individuals who guide us, support us, and help us pursue our goals and passions. They can offer us advice, encouragement, and opportunities to develop our skills and interests.

Role models are individuals we admire and aspire to emulate. They can be a source of inspiration and motivation by successfully expressing their passions and goals. The role models in our lives can help us form a clear picture of what is possible and inspire us to pursue our passions.

Community and culture

Our community and culture play an essential role in shaping our passions through the values, norms, and opportunities they offer. Our community and culture can provide an environment of support and encouragement for living out our passions by promoting creativity, self-expression, and self-confidence.

In addition, our community and culture can also have an impact on our perceptions of what an acceptable career or lifestyle is. For example, a community that values a particular career or profession might encourage it to pursue a passion for that career. On the other hand, a community that promotes a broad range of interests and activities can help us develop and explore a wide range of passions.

Education and Learning Experiences

Education and learning experiences play an essential role in developing our passions through exposure to new ideas, knowledge, and skills. Our education system and learning experiences can provide an environment of discovery and experimentation, helping us identify and develop our interests and passions.

In addition, our educational experiences can expose us to mentors, role models, and opportunities for growth and development. Our learning experiences can help us develop a passion for a specific subject area or activity by fostering creativity, problem-solving, and critical thinking.

Work Environment

Our work environment plays a crucial role in living out our passions through the opportunities and challenges they present. A positive work environment can inspire and motivate living out our passions by promoting creativity, self-expression, and career development.

In addition, our work environment can also have an impact on our emotional well-being and happiness. A work environment that is supportive and encouraging can encourage us to pursue our passions and experience a sense of fulfillment and meaning in our careers.

Concluding view

The social influences on passion are manifold and diverse, and they play a critical role in the emergence, formation, and expression of our passions. Our family, friends, mentors, community, and culture shape the social environment where we discover, develop, and live out our passions. By acknowledging and appreciating the influences of these social factors, we can better understand their role in our life's journey toward self-discovery and fulfillment.

The Emerging Movement of Passion-Driven Companies: A New Paradigm in the World of Work

The business world is experiencing an exciting transformation, where companies are beginning to recognize the importance of passion in the work environment and encouraging employees to live out their passions, even if it is diametrically opposed to the current status quo. This new approach to the work environment has significantly impacted the performance, employee engagement, and business growth of companies worldwide. In this Chapter, we will explore the rise of these passion-driven companies, discuss examples of successful implementations, and examine the steadfastness of this approach.

The Paradigm Shift to Passion-Driven Companies

Traditionally, work environments often target task execution, profit maximization, and corporate goals. However, this approach can lead to a lack of employee engagement, creativity, and an overall decline in the work environment's positive impact on employees' lives. In response, a new paradigm emerged - the passion-driven company.

Passion-driven companies recognize the importance of passion in the work environment and encourage employees to pursue it, even if it goes against the current status quo. These companies are focused on creating an environment where employees are inspired and motivated and can reach their full potential by living out their passions.

Examples of Successful Implementations

1. **Google**: Google is a prime example of a passion-driven company. The company encourages employees to pursue their passions through projects like Google's 20% project, where employees can spend 20% of their time on personal projects that address their passions. This approach has led to many

successful product innovations, including Gmail and Google News.

2. **Zappos**: Online detail retailer Zappos has a passionate approach to customer service and culture. The company encourages employees to bring their unique passions and interests to their work, leading to a culture of creativity, innovation, and world-class customer service.

3. **Patagonia**: Patagonia is a well-known outdoor light company passionate about the environment and conservation. The company encourages employees to pursue their passions for the environment, which has led to several initiatives that promote environmental conservation.

These examples illustrate how passion-driven companies can be successful by encouraging employees to pursue their passions and reach their full potential.

The Impact on Business Growth

Implementing a passion-driven approach can have a direct impact on business growth. When employees are encouraged to pursue their passions, it increases employee engagement, creativity, and productivity. These factors, in turn, can lead to improved company performance, greater customer satisfaction, and, ultimately, business growth.

In addition, creating a positive work environment where passion is encouraged can increase employee retention and attract top talent. This can give a company a competitive edge in the yard business and help attract the best and most talented employees.

The Persistence of Passion-Driven Companies

One of the most remarkable qualities of passion-driven companies is their steadfastness. These companies focus not only on short-term profits or corporate goals but also on creating a durable and positive work environment for employees. This approach has the potential to ensure long-term success and persistence, as employees are happy and motivated to produce their best work.

In addition, the steadfastness of a passion-driven company can also lead to increased company fidelity among employees and customers. When employees and customers have a strong emotional connection to a company because of its passion and values, they are likelier to remain loyal and support the company over the long term.

The Future of Passion-Driven Companies

The future of passion-driven companies looks bright. These companies will play an ever-increasing role in the business world due to the growing recognition of the importance of passion in the work environment.

Companies that adopt a passion-driven approach can expect to have an edge in employee engagement, creativity, and business growth.

In a world where the work environment is becoming ever more industrialized and automated, the human element of passion will play a critical role in the success of companies.

These companies will be constantly looking for ways to cultivate and support their employees' passion as it directly impacts the performance and success of the company as a whole.

Conclusion

Passion-driven companies represent a new paradigm in the business world, where the importance of passion in the world of work is recognized and encouraged.

These companies have significantly impacted the business world, business growth, and employee engagement. With a growing focus on the importance of passion, we can expect these companies to play a more significant role in the future business world and positively impact the lives of their employees and customers.

Don't miss out!

Visit the website below and you can sign up to receive emails whenever Carl Davis publishes a new book. There's no charge and no obligation.

https://books2read.com/r/B-A-ZAXZ-XXAYC

BOOKS 2 READ

Connecting independent readers to independent writers.

Also by Carl Davis

Ek, is Dawid Soeker
A Brief History Of Christianity In Africa
Icing the Eskimo - The Art of Aggressive Sales
Introduction to Pastoral Counselling
Nuclear Faith
Toxic Pulpit
Van Paradegrond tot Pastorie
Group Dynamics and Motivation
Introduction to Leadership and Management
Pastoral counselling models for perinatal and postpartum episodes
Basic New Testament Survey
Help! I'm managing personnel
So......You want to be a Waiter
The Art of Preaching
Eternal Logos: The Evolution of Scriptural Interpretation: From
Ancient Methodology to Postmodern Perspectives
Ewige Woord Die Evolusie van Skrifuitleg: Van Antieke Metodiek tot
Postmoderne Perspektiewe
Teaching Ministry
The Funny Side Of Reasoning - Fallacies, principles and typologies in
the modern business world.
Passion Unleashed: Igniting The Future With Purpose.

About the Author

Carl Davis holds a Doctorate in Missiology based upon research of Organizational Growth in the Post Modern Society.I started my work life serving in the South African Defence Force – first at the Recruiting Division, then moving to a Medical Command where I served as a Generalist Personnel Officer. For the last two years of my service, I was tasked with the Personnel management of the Integration process, inclusive of entrance and exit strategies.After honorable discharge after more than 10 years in the South African Defence Force, I took up the post of Managing Director of a Non-Government Organization, established to uplift impoverished communities in and around Potchefstroom, while also appointed as a part-time lecturer of undergraduates (specifically on leadership).Three years later I was appointed as Rector, managing an Educational Institute with 4000 students spread over 36 African countries. While in this position I had the opportunity to lecture extensively abroad and published various articles on leadership; with specific emphasis on motivation and group dynamics. I am a strong believer in utilizing a blended and integrated approach in all of the training (including the new material which I developed) I developed which included – Leadership (within a Faith based community), andragogy, and Cultural Diversity management.I am also a graduate of the University of Stellenbosch's Facilitative Leadership Programme (BUVTON), consulting and facilitating with organizations that are "stuck" (- Alice Mann 1998-) specifically in the process of change management.